I Love You More Than Mountains

BY KRISTEN EMILY BEHL

ILLUSTRATED BY MONICA PATERSON

CAN YOU IDENTIFY ALL **17** NATIONAL PARKS INSIDE?

© 2021 Kristen Emily Behl
All rights reserved. No part of this book may be reproduced in any form without permission from the author.

ISBN:
e-Book: 978-1-954809-04-8
Paperback: 978-1-954809-05-5
Hardcover: 978-1-954809-06-2

Published by Goose Water Press LLC.
www.kristenemilybehl.com
For bulk orders, please contact publisher directly at connect@kristenemilybehl.com.

To my daughters and their daddy -
my favorite adventurers

and taller than the trees.

I love you drier than the desert

and wider than the seas.

and darker than the caves.

and louder than the waves.

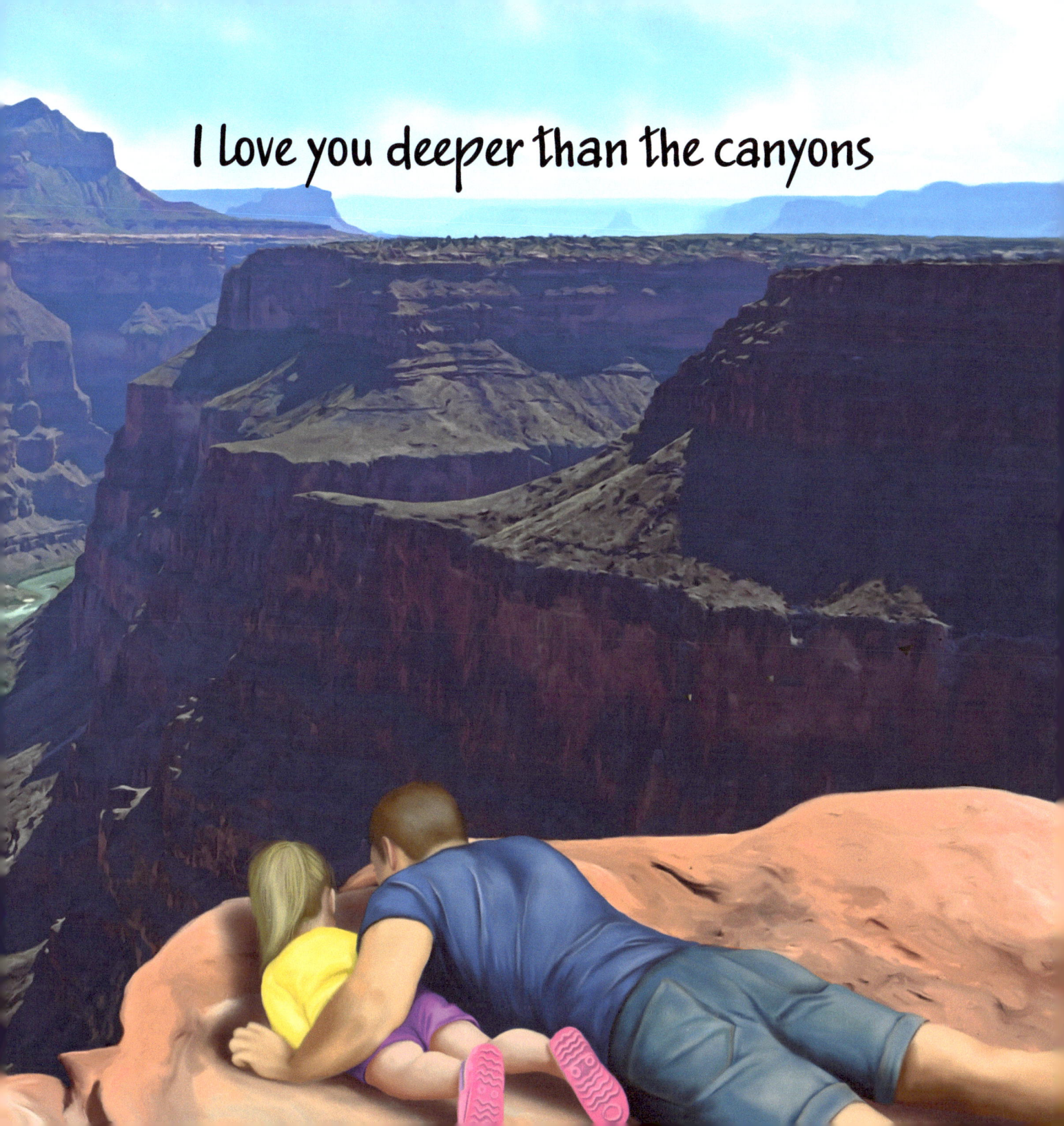

and cooler than the stream.

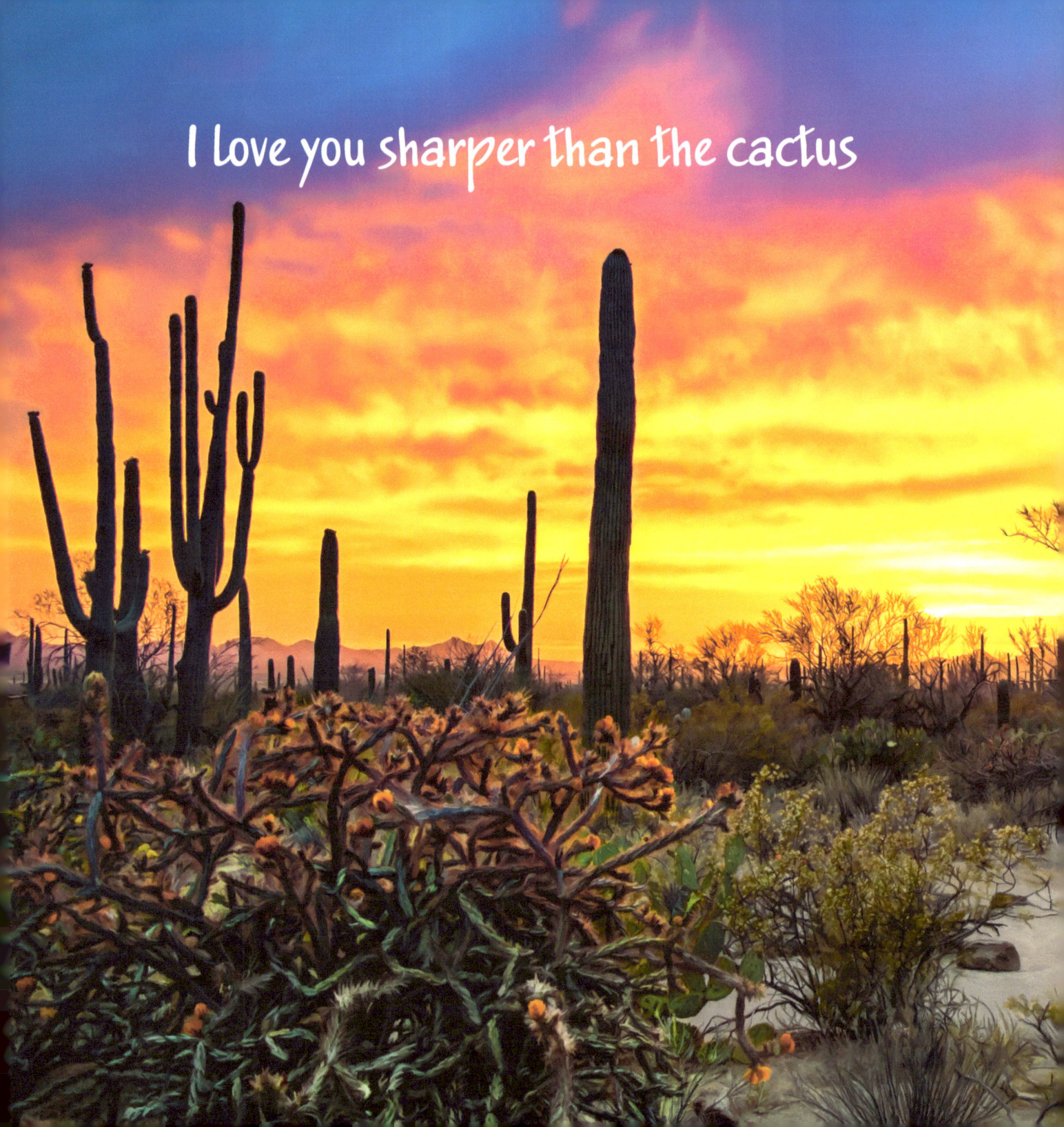

and hotter than the steam.

You are lovelier than northern lights,

bright shining as can be.

About the Author

Kristen Emily Behl lives in the midwestern U.S. with her husband and two young girls. Taking care of her kids reignited her childhood passion for writing and led her to create Goose Water Press, a small publishing company through which she produces children's picture books and adult non-fiction, all centered around building up families. She and her husband take advantage of every opportunity to road trip across their beautiful nation and explore God's creation with the kids. In just three years, their toddlers have visited 14 national parks! "I love you more than mountains" is a phrase her husband frequently says to their girls, and thus sparked the idea for this book.

About the Illustrator

Monica is native to South Africa. Together with her supportive hubby, she has raised three young men who share her talent for creativity.
She is an artist who draws inspiration from the many different places and cultures she has experienced. Having settled down in the UK, Monica is now able to focus on one of her lifelong dreams of illustrating children's books.

Please leave a review! This helps other prospective readers immensely.

Don't miss these titles by Kristen Emily Behl!

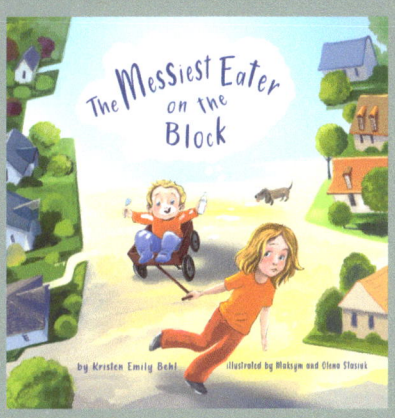 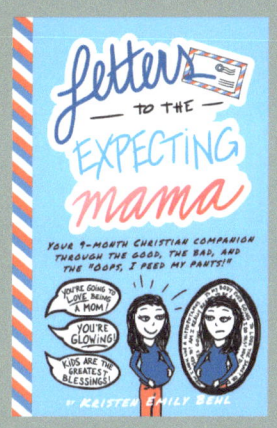

The Messiest Eater on the Block

A frustrated older sister tells her perspective of a little brother with such poor table manners that unwanted dinner guests begin showing up at the door. Get ready to make silly sounds and use your imagination as the young messy eaters in your family learn that they are loved despite–or because of–the messes.

Letters to the Expecting Mama

A book that feels like a series of personal letters from a friend, designed to progress with you through your pregnancy one exciting month at a time. Your source of practical advice, Christian love and encouragement, candid truths, and comic relief.

www.kristenemilybehl.com

@goosewaterpress

Did you guess the National Parks?

Cover: Grand Teton NP
Yosemite NP
Sequoia NP
Joshua Tree NP
Olympic NP
Zion NP
Carlsbad Caverns NP
Glacier NP **
Acadia NP

Grand Canyon NP
Great Smoky Mountain NP
Saguaro NP
Yellowstone NP
Denali NP *
Hawaii Volcanoes NP *
Arches NP
Rocky Mountain NP

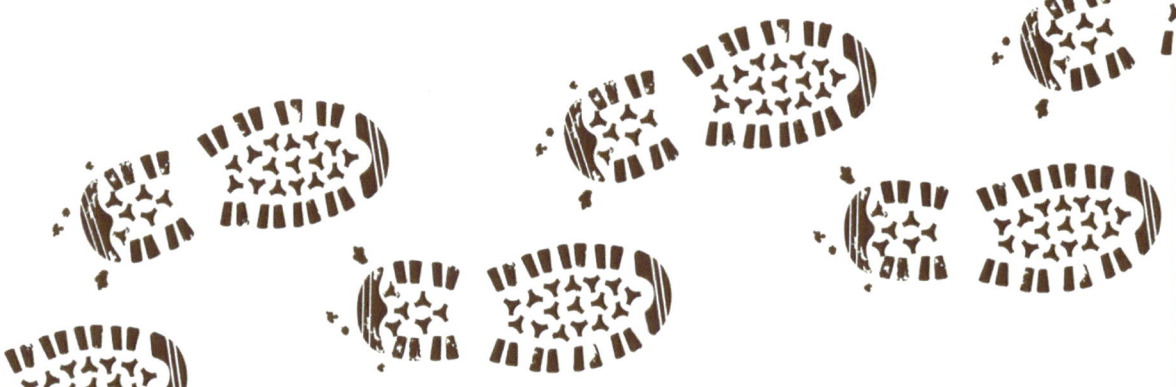

All images used in the creation of the illustrations are credited to Adobe Stock, with the exception of:
*NP Gallery
**Permission by tunisiebooking.com